LITHA
THE SUMMER SOLSTICE

Amy Cesari

Be a fire-safe witch!

Lots of space above and around the flame.

Candle is on a fire-safe dish.

Never leave flames unattended.

COPYRIGHT & GENERAL DISCLAIMER:
LITHA THE SUMMER SOLSTICE
ALL TEXT AND IMAGES © 2017-2025 BOOK OF SHADOWS LLC, AMY CESARI

THIS BOOK DOES NOT CONTAIN MEDICAL ADVICE AND DOES NOT INTEND TO TREAT OR DIAGNOSE MEDICAL OR HEALTH ISSUES. ALWAYS SEEK PROFESSIONAL MEDICAL TREATMENT. AND DON'T EAT OR USE PLANTS IF YOU DON'T KNOW WHAT THEY ARE.

ALL RIGHTS RESERVED. For personal use only. No parts of this book may be reproduced, copied, or transmitted in any form, by any means, including photocopying, recording, or other electronic or mechanical methods, without the prior written permission of the author, except in the case of brief quotations for critical reviews and certain other noncommercial uses permitted by copyright law.

DISCLAIMER OF LIABILITY: This book is for informational and entertainment purposes only and is not intended as a substitute for medical, financial, spiritual, or life advice of any kind. Like any craft involving flames, the power of your mind unhinged, eating plants and herbs, and the unyielding forces of the universe, Witchcraft poses some inherent risk. The author and publisher are not liable or responsible for any outcome of magical spells performed from this book or otherwise. Readers agree to cast spells, work with fire, ingest herbs, soak in bath salts, light candles and incense, channel deities, use spirit boards, and perform any and all other magical practices at their own risk. The images in this book are for decorative purposes—they are not realistic guides for arranging flame-based altars. Always place a fireproof dish beneath candles & incense. Leave clearance above & around flames. Do not place flammable objects near flames and never leave flaming things or incense unattended. Readers of this book take full responsibility when using fire. Readers accept full personal risk and responsibility for the outcome, consequence, and magic of any spells they cast. This book is not for children. And so it shall be.

This Book Belongs To:

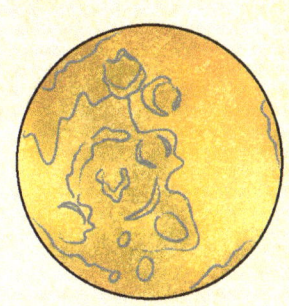

What is Litha?

Midsummer, also known as Litha and the Summer Solstice, marks the longest day of the year. It is an ancient seasonal celebration of the sun's full strength.

The sun symbolizes the light and life of a higher power, the light within yourself, and an elevated realm of consciousness.

The full light of Litha is a powerful time to allow the abundance of light and the empowerment of your most vibrant self.

Litha is celebrated approximately June 21 in the northern hemisphere of earth, which corresponds seasonally to December 21st in the southern hemisphere of earth.

About this Book

Magic is not something just to read about. Magic must be practiced and experienced first-hand.

The blank pages in this book have been placed purposefully. They are for you to learn, to discover, to explore, and to fill with your own magic.

Consider writing spells, recipes, rituals, traditions, and intentions that you experience and discover as you practice magic on the summer solstice.

When you take the time to practice magic and write your own experiences, the solstice will become real and alive within you.

The seasons or the "Wheel of the Year" relate to the cycles, tilt, and planetary motion right here on Earth. Ancient Celts celebrated these seasonal shifts and used them for magic and ritual, as noted on the chart above. The moon shares a shorter, corresponding cycle, which completes in 28 days instead of 365 days in a year.

SOUTHERN HEMISPHERE SEASONS: If you're on the "southern" half of the Earth, like in Australia, the seasonal shifts are opposite. So you'll feel the energy of the summer solstice (corresponding to the full moon) in December instead of June.

A Note About the Cross-Quarter Dates: The dates for the two solstices and two equinoxes each year—Ostara, Litha, Mabon, and Yule—are calculated astronomically from the position of the Earth to the sun. The "cross-quarter" festivals, which are the points between —Imbolc, Beltane, Lughnasadh, and Samhain—are often celebrated on "fixed" dates instead of the actual midpoints. It's more common to celebrate on "fixed festival dates." Choose either date or any time in between for your own festivities or ritual. 'Tis the season for magic.

HISTORY
OF LITHA
& THE SUMMER SOLSTICE

Litha is the celebration of the longest day and shortest night of the year, a time when the sun reaches its peak power.

"Solstice" comes from the Latin word "solstitium," meaning "Sun stands still"—as the sun sets at approximately the same point for six days at the solstices. And the word "Litha" is a modern interpretation that likely originated from an Anglo-Saxon word describing midsummer and the month of June.

Across the globe, many cultures have honored this celestial turning point with fire, feasts, and rituals to connect to divine powers and the ever-turning cycles of nature.

In Britain and Europe, Midsummer was and is a time for fire festivals, feasting, and honoring the spirits of nature.

In China, the solstices are associated with the balance of yin and yang. The winter solstice honors the return of yang (active masculine energy), while the summer solstice celebrates the peak of yin (receptive feminine energy), which is often connected to the Earth and the energy of fertility.

Indigenous American people also have legends and rituals of the summer solstice, with sacred ceremonies to honor Sun Gods, Earth Spirits, and the Great Spirit.

Eastern European traditions include Kupala Night, where people celebrate with ceremonial fire jumping, love divinations in which flower wreaths are floated down rivers, and bathing rituals to cleanse the spirit.

Although ancient cultures each marked this sacred time in their own ways, the similarities between them all point to the sun, the divine, and the acceptance and reverence of the inevitable cycles of life.

Several ancient artifacts and legends depict a horse pulling a sun in a cart, such as the Nordic Trundholm Sun Chariot.

HISTORY
OF LITHA
& THE SUMMER SOLSTICE

There are megaliths, temples, and stone carvings all over the world that align with the placement of the sun on the solstice.

These similarities point to the importance of the sun's passage and cycles for our ancient ancestors. Around the world, the solstice was seen as a liminal time—when the veil between worlds grew thin, and spirits roamed freely.

The summer solstice sun blessed the earth with its power, yet also peaked and began its inevitable descent into winter. From grand temples to small village bonfires, ancient people saw this day as one of both celebration and reflection on the ever-turning cycles of life and death. Here are a few of many "sun temples" that still remain:

At Stonehenge in Wiltshire, UK, the most well-known of these megaliths, you can witness the sunrise on the summer solstice aligning perfectly within the stone circle.

In Egypt, if you stand to the east of the Sphinx on the summer solstice, the sunset shines exactly between the two largest of the Great Pyramids.

Angkor Wat Temple in Cambodia is also aligned with the movement of the sun, and you can witness the sunrise at midsummer aligning with the temple's western gate.

The Ancestral Pueblo people of North America carved petroglyphs at Chaco Canyon (modern-day New Mexico) to mark the passage of the sun through the solstices and equinoxes.

Wyoming's Bighorn Medicine Wheel is an ancient limestone structure that aligns with the solstices. It demonstrates the deep connection and importance of the sun and celestial cycles to indigenous North American people.

And the Mayan City of Chichen Itza also has architectural elements that align with the solstices and equinoxes.

Ancient stone monuments signify the "marriage of heaven and earth," aligning the cosmos with our earthly realm.

LEGENDS OF SUN & FIRE

The summer solstice has long been a time of fire, radiance, and divine power, inspiring myths of sun gods, fire spirits, and celestial battles. Legends of the sun across cultures around the globe have solidified the solstice as a time of strength, transformation, and magic.

In Egyptian mythology, the sun was the god Ra. He sailed across the sky in his boat, defeated Apep (the force of chaos) in serpent form, and ensured that light prevailed on Earth. Ra's strong presence at Midsummer symbolized the triumph of order over darkness, a cycle that would eventually turn as the sun's strength waned. Ra's stories are also thought to be allegories about the journey of the human soul.

The Greek legend of Helios, a charioteer who drove the sun across the sky, also ties into solstice themes. His son, Phaethon, once tried to drive his father's chariot but lost control, scorching the Earth and nearly destroying the world. Zeus struck him down with a lightning bolt, saving the Earth and reminding mortals to respect the sun's immense power.

Among Norse legends, the solstice is associated with Surtr, the fire giant who engulfed the world in flames at Ragnarok. Solstice bonfires are lit to honor the element of fire, both as a force of protection and an omen of the cycle of destruction and rebirth.

In Hindu tradition, the sun god Surya is revered as a giver of life and cosmic order. The solstice marks a shift in his journey, a time of great solar energy, making it ideal for prayers, purification, and devotion.

Legends of sun and fire remind us that the solstice is not just about light—it is about power, transformation, and the eternal dance between dark and light, creation and destruction. In its eternal dance, the sun burns brightly before it turns to darkness yet again.

LEGENDS
OF THE BATTLE OF
LIGHT AND DARK

The summer solstice is the pinnacle of light, yet hidden within its brilliance is the turn of the wheel towards darkness. Many traditions see this time not just as a celebration of the sun's peak but as the moment when the balance begins to tip—the inevitable turning of the wheel from fiery power to the quiet of shadow.

In Celtic and Norse traditions, this shift is embodied in the battle between the Oak King and the Holly King. The Oak King, (ruler of the light half of the year), reaches the height of his power at the summer solstice, growing in strength as the days have lengthened. The Holly King (ruler of the dark half of the year) regains his power at the autumn equinox, signaling the return of the darkness. Though the Oak King has reached his peak at the summer solstice, his power will now begin to fade.

A similar battle exists in Hindu mythology, where the solstice marks the transition into Dakshinayana, the period of time between the summer and winter solstice. This is a time of introspection, when spiritual pursuits are emphasized over worldly success.

In Slavic folklore, Midsummer's Eve is a night of fiery battles between good and evil forces, where spirits roam and humans light bonfires to ward off misfortune. Fire-jumping rituals symbolize the triumph of light over darkness, but also acknowledge the presence of unseen forces and inevitable cycles moving beneath the surface.

The solstice reminds us that no light burns forever without rest. This is not a loss, but a never-ending cycle—a lesson that in every triumph, the seeds of transformation are already taking root.

Holly King & Oak King

There are many other notable pairs of dark and light legends, such as Baldur & Hodur, and Sol & Mani.

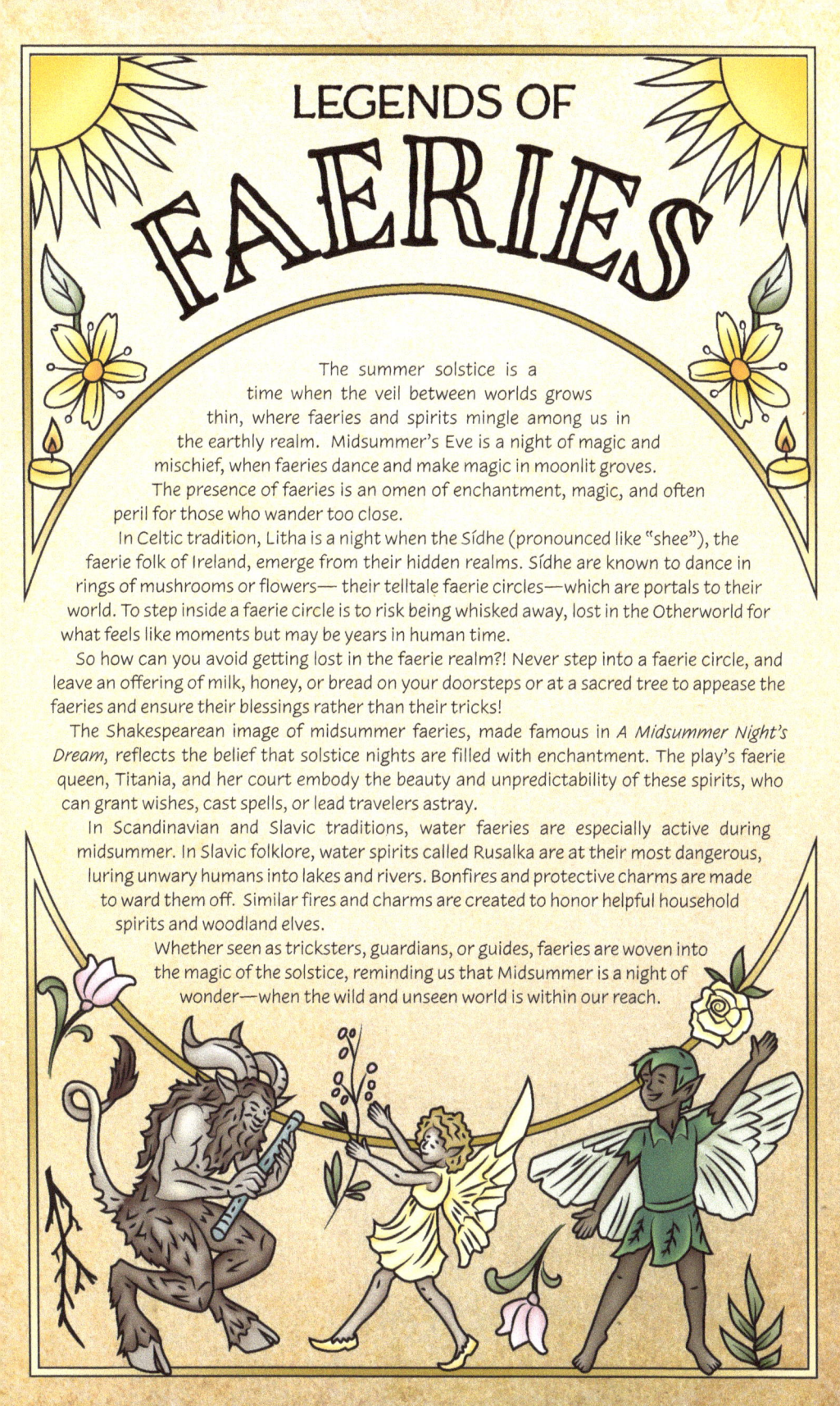

LEGENDS OF FAERIES

The summer solstice is a time when the veil between worlds grows thin, where faeries and spirits mingle among us in the earthly realm. Midsummer's Eve is a night of magic and mischief, when faeries dance and make magic in moonlit groves. The presence of faeries is an omen of enchantment, magic, and often peril for those who wander too close.

In Celtic tradition, Litha is a night when the Sídhe (pronounced like "shee"), the faerie folk of Ireland, emerge from their hidden realms. Sídhe are known to dance in rings of mushrooms or flowers— their telltale faerie circles—which are portals to their world. To step inside a faerie circle is to risk being whisked away, lost in the Otherworld for what feels like moments but may be years in human time.

So how can you avoid getting lost in the faerie realm?! Never step into a faerie circle, and leave an offering of milk, honey, or bread on your doorsteps or at a sacred tree to appease the faeries and ensure their blessings rather than their tricks!

The Shakespearean image of midsummer faeries, made famous in *A Midsummer Night's Dream,* reflects the belief that solstice nights are filled with enchantment. The play's faerie queen, Titania, and her court embody the beauty and unpredictability of these spirits, who can grant wishes, cast spells, or lead travelers astray.

In Scandinavian and Slavic traditions, water faeries are especially active during midsummer. In Slavic folklore, water spirits called Rusalka are at their most dangerous, luring unwary humans into lakes and rivers. Bonfires and protective charms are made to ward them off. Similar fires and charms are created to honor helpful household spirits and woodland elves.

Whether seen as tricksters, guardians, or guides, faeries are woven into the magic of the solstice, reminding us that Midsummer is a night of wonder—when the wild and unseen world is within our reach.

Hold citrine to your heart or solar plexus to know your desires and inner wisdom.

Burn incense with bergamot, goldenrod, rose, and thyme for an uplifting boost.

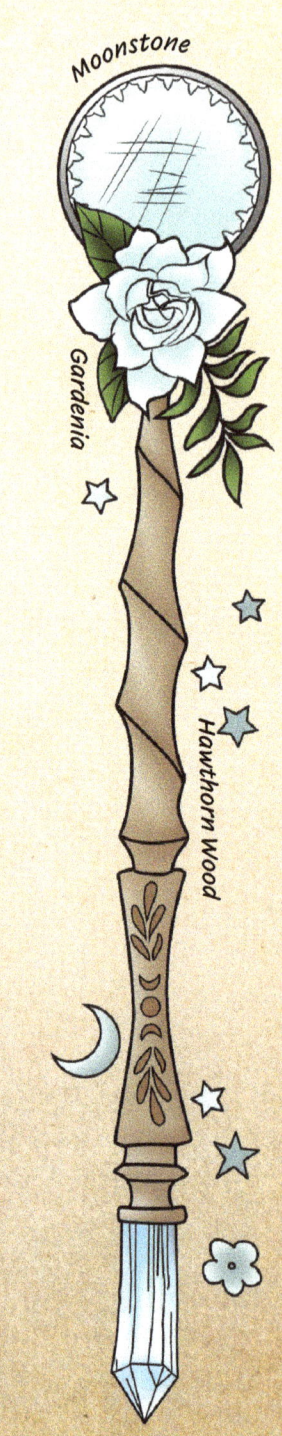

- Moth -
Traveling between light and dark

Bathe with lavender and peony petals to enhance your psychic powers and manifest your wishes.

Burn rose geranium, sweet woodruff, or star anise to connect with fire energy.

Ground yourself with earthy incense like patchouli, cypress, or vetivert root.

Feel the magic of the sun. Remember that you can change, grow, and live a bright life by working with herbs like cinquefoil, woodruff, and cinnamon.

Creating a Litha Altar
Centering Your Magical Focus and Intentions

Creating a seasonal altar is a powerful way to center your sabbat celebration.

An altar is a place to bring the spiritual into the material world—As Above, So Below. Altars speak to your subconscious in a way that's deeper than words or rational thought. This can help uncover feelings or powers within yourself that may be indescribable, and will set the stage to inspire magic and ritual in life.

To create an altar that represents the energy of the summer solstice, collect a few items that evoke the sun or summer to you—herbs, crystals, symbols, deities, candles, or things you've crafted or created.

For a more balanced traditional altar, place statuary or representations of the "masculine" god and "feminine" goddess—these can be the Sun and Moon or deities of your choice or calling. Then add representations of the four elements, a bowl of water, candles for fire, salt or a small plant for earth, and incense or aromatic flowers for the element of air.

Of course, these are just ideas. While it's fine to look outward for inspiration, listen to the language of your soul and pick colors, scents, deities, and symbols that are uniquely yours.

Consecrate your altar with incense, candle flames, moonwater, or aromatic oils. As you do so, take a moment to feel gratitude for the things in your life that are illuminated or already present. Then feel gratitude for your wishes, dreams, and desires that are yet to come.

Let your Litha altar be a place of power and reflection for the turning of the season, helping you harness the energies of the sun, inspire your magical workings, and center and focus the growth and fulfillment you desire in the coming months.

Hang St. John's Wort over your door or place it on your altar to bring happiness to your home.

HERBCRAFT & HARVEST
THE MAGICAL CONNECTION BETWEEN EARTH AND SUN

Many summer solstice traditions touch upon the life-giving connection between the sun and earth, as the abundance of plant life on our planet depends upon the light of the sun to grow and thrive.

Here are a few simple and joyful ways to connect with this magical season through traditional folk crafts and herbs.

Harvesting Herbs: Litha is a powerful and traditional time to gather herbs, as they are at their "most magical" when the sun is at its peak. Herbs like St. John's wort, lavender, and sage are full of energy from the long sunny days. Gather them at noon for the most potent magical effects.

Charm Bags: Once you've harvested and dried your herbs, why not turn them into charm bags? These little pouches are perfect for carrying the magic of the solstice with you into the coming months. Combine herbs like chamomile for relaxation, lavender for protection, and mint for energy. Place them in a small bag as you set your intentions, feeling into the energy of each herb.

Creating Solar Water: Place a bowl of water and herbs under the sun to create solar water. This water will absorb the sun's fiery energy. Use it to water your plants or as a base for spells and potions that need a little extra sunshine.

Decorating: Use your harvested herbs and flowers to decorate your home. Tie bundles of herbs with twine and hang them around your house or above your door. Not only will they look festive, they'll also fill your home with delightful natural scents and magic. They'll also be preserved for later use as they dry... practical magic at its finest.

- Ouroboros -
The eternal cycle of life, death, and rebirth.

Circle & Spiral Dancing
A Tradition to Move with the Cycles of Life

Circle and spiral dancing are joyful, traditional ways to celebrate and connect with the natural rhythms of life. These dances are deeply symbolic, representing our place in the cycles of the seasons and the continuous flow of energy in the universe.

1. Gather a group, or go at it alone.
2. Prepare some joyful music or a simple chant to go with the dance. You might like to play traditional Celtic music, but anything lively that uplifts the spirit will work.
3. If you're in a group, form a circle by holding hands. The circle represents unity and eternity—a never-ending loop that connects us all. If you're alone, just imagine a circle of energy and light radiating around you.

Circle Dance: For the summer solstice, you might like to circle clock-wise or sun-wise, representing the movement of the sun. This dance is simple—just travel in a circle. The key is to move as one in a group, feeling each other's energy as you step together, or feeling the sensation in your own body if you are alone.

Spiral Dance: A spiral dance starts with the lead dancer turning inward and walking towards the center, with each person following until the circle winds into a tight spiral. This movement symbolizes drawing energy inwards. Then unwind and release by reversing your steps, unwinding the spiral back into a circle. This represents releasing the gathered energy.

Close your dance ritual: End your dance with a moment of cheer and gratitude for the joy of the dance of life.

Lemon
Purification, the Sun, & Life

Litha Spells

The Summer Solstice
Celebrating the Longest Day of the Year

The sun reaches its highest point and power at noon on the summer solstice, marking a powerful shift from light to dark. It's an "in-between" time, a chance to slip into another world and change the course of your future.

The sun represents the self. This is a time where you can see and connect clearly with your own true "you" and the height of your personal power.

It's a magical day, so why not experience the longest day of the year at its fullest — from dawn to noon to sundown?

At Sunrise: In ancient times, many cultures built temples to catch the first rays of sun on the summer solstice—such as Stonehenge. Familiarize yourself with when and where the first rays of sun will hit your yard or favorite outdoor location.

As the first ray of sun arrives, ring bells, yell, chant, sing, and welcome the light.

Or meditate with your eyes closed to get in touch with your inner light as you feel the sun's first rays.

At Noon: Make a positive choice or a change for yourself. If something has been holding you back or feeling "wrong," cast a spell and declare that you are going to make a change for the better. The doors to any other life or situation you desire are open. Take this opportunity to walk through.

At Sunset: Do some divination! Set up a candlelit tarot table—outside at sunset if you can. Get a cup of honey-whiskey or tea with lemon and honey—and pull some tarot cards. Ask questions to guide you towards the fulfillment of your highest self and to discover the purpose of your soul.

Litha Spells

Receiving With Grace
And The Magic of Litha's Bright Light

The light of abundance and blessings of the sun are always shining on you—but are you allowing yourself to receive them?

Midsummer, or Litha, marks the longest day of the year and is the celebration of the sun's full strength. The sun at Litha allows us to see many things we normally can't or don't want to see, like turning on a bright light and suddenly realizing there's dust everywhere.

The darkest shadows also fall from the brightest lights—a powerful duality.

One of the common personal "shadows" you might uncover in yourself is resistance to receiving. You may want or need something, but when it comes time to receive it—perhaps you freak out and step back because of guilt, insecurity, or fear of your own success. Sound familiar?

The full light of Litha is a powerful time to allow the abundance of light and the empowerment of your most vibrant self.

The magic is in receiving—but does that feel hard? Do you want to work for it or petition your deity on your knees in an elaborate ritual before you can have your blessings?

PREPARE: Pick flowers ethically or buy a small bouquet from a local farm or seller. Create a mandala (circular pattern) with the flowers and tea lights, leaving room to place a deck of tarot cards or a small notebook in the middle.

Light the candles, then pull three tarot cards to "shine a light" on how you can easily receive what you need in abundance. Alternately, after the candle has shone on the notebook, free-write on its pages and allow your subconscious to tell you the same.

A Magical Garden
Sow the Seeds for An Autumn Harvest

There's still time to plant a magical garden in early June, and with a little love from you and the power of the elements, you can enjoy a bountiful harvest come Autumn.

PLANTING RITUALS: As you till the soil, release any old patterns or bits that you wish to discard. Feel it all grounding into the earth. Burn incense or drink a bitter tea such as kava.

With each seed that you plant, set an intention for what you desire. As you tend to the seeds in the coming weeks, feel the energy of their growth. Watch them take root and witness the sense of sacred power that breathes life into all things. Feel that same power inside of yourself and imagine however you wish to be. In time, you'll find that you connect to your magic whenever you tend to your garden.

THINGS TO PLANT IN EARLY JUNE

A PUMPKIN PATCH: If you've got the space and sun, growing pumpkins is a magical experience. Plant your seeds by the first week of June and they'll be ready to harvest by Mabon.

VEGGIES & HERBS: You're more likely to eat your witchy veggies if you grow them yourself!

For shadier spots, try lettuce, broccoli, spinach, small cabbages, carrots, kale, and parsnips.

For sunnier spots, try basil, mustard, oregano, chives, thyme, sage, cucumber, squash, melon, beets, pumpkins, and turnips.

FLOWERS: You can still plant some flowers to harvest in fall—just in time for your Mabon altar and spellwork. Try sunflowers, zinnias, cosmos, nasturtiums, cornflower (bachelor buttons), and other wildflowers indigenous to your region.

Faerie and Flower Magic
Harness the Playful Energy of Summer

Litha is a traditional night for faerie magic, so why not invite the faeries to join you?

PREPARE: Wreaths, garlands, and bouquets will set a magical mood. Flowers and strong herbs represent the full strength of the sun and the power of the solstice. Craft wreaths or garlands with fennel, St. John's Wort, white lilies, rowan, or other plants in green, white, gold, and yellow.

Light candles, flowery incense, or oil lamps mixed with essential oils. Make a treat for the faeries such as a lemon and elderflower cake—faeries love elderflower.

Consider serving dandelion or white wine, lemonade, honey-whiskey, or herbal tonics.

INVITE THE FAERIES: To call an earth faerie (gnomes, brownies, and tree spirits) bury a crystal partially in the ground at dawn. Chant something like, *"Faeries of the Earth and Trees, join this ritual, if you please."*

Then watch closely for faeries to appear. Earth faeries may like to participate in divination to awaken your awareness to the spirit world.

To call air faeries like sylphs (the winged ones), spin around three times clockwise at sunset as you toss flower petals or herbs into the air. Then lay on the ground and look up at the sky. Chant, *"Spirits of the air, can you hear me? Are you there?"* Air faeries may like to participate in divination or magic to awaken your creativity and inspiration.

Enhance your chances of seeing faeries with wild thyme or fern seeds. Ancient legends say to rub these herbs on your eyelids, but use caution with this method!

Faerie Garden Party
A Celebration of Midsummer

Made famous by Shakespeare and centuries of folklore, Litha is a time where the faeries emerge. It's the faerie holiday for celebrating and also causing mischief to humans, a bit like a faerie trick-or-treat. According to legend, the faeries play tricks, and humans are supposed to offer treats to pacify them.

A Midsummer faerie garden party or Litha ritual is an enchanting way to celebrate the wild, carefree energy of summer and to give the faeries something sweet so they don't play any tricks.

Decorate your garden with faerie lights and set up an outdoor altar with an offering to the faeries. They love honey, flowers, herbs, sweets, and cake.

You can write poetry praising them, sing songs, play music, make drawings or other crafts in their honor, like corn-husk dolls with fairy wings and tiny flower crowns.

If you're more outdoorsy, you can play lively, lighthearted games and sports or go foraging for herbs and wildflowers, bringing some back for the faerie altar, of course!

Make sure to research the intricacies of faeries more thoroughly before you start working with them because they can be quite tricky and mischievous.

Never play tricks on faeries and always make sure to thank them for their presence.

Give them sweet flowery offerings and keep your garden full of energy and life to delight them and make them happy.

Drawing Down the Sun
A Ritual To Harness The Sun's Energy

"Drawing Down the Sun" was traditionally done by priests while "Drawing Down the Moon" was done by priestesses, but nowadays, anyone can (and should!) harness the powers of both the sun and the moon.

If you don't want to channel the sun as a god or goddess, you can channel it as abundance, creative energy, light energy, life energy, or whatever is meaningful.

PREPARE: Plan to do this ritual in the sun, preferably at noon, at the peak of the sun, or anytime while the sun is still shining. You'll need a crystal—quartz, crackle quartz, sunstone, or red tourmaline are all good choices. You can also use a candle or some flowers, or just use yourself and the sun with no tools or extra items. Set up a small altar for your crystal, candle, and other supplies.

DOING THE SPELL: Sit or stand in the sun, holding your crystal. Of course, don't look directly at the sun. You might like to close your eyes. Feel the earth's energy grounding you down, coming up from the earth and supplying you with power and steadiness.

Then feel the sun's energy powering you up. Channel it through you and let it shine back out. Visualize a bright light coming out from the center of yourself and into a sphere around you. Feel it growing larger and larger.

Thank the sun for its energy and light. Make sure to ground out again and don't sit in the hot sun too long.

Handfasting
A Celtic Marriage Tradition

Handfasting is a Celtic ritual that symbolizes the binding together of two lives. It is often performed outdoors, connected to nature.

You might like to gather your loved ones for this ritual. However, it can be done in private with just you and your partner.

The centerpiece of the handfasting is the cord itself, which can be made from various materials like ribbons, strips cut from meaningful garments, or natural vines or flower chains. Choose colors that symbolize your wishes for the marriage (red for passion, green for growth, etc.) or coordinate it to your wedding decor.

The actual handfasting can be done at any point of a modern wedding ceremony. You can perform it during your vows, before, or after.

To perform the handfasting, stand with your partner and hold hands, either facing each other or side-by-side. An officiant can drape and tie the cord over your hands, or you and your partner can each wrap one end of the cord with a free hand. You can choose to hold just one hand of your partner and tie two hands together or do a double-hand hold. These variations are up to you and the mood of your wedding. Choose what feels right in the flow of your ceremony.

Once the cord is tied, it's time to celebrate! Some couples choose to conclude the ceremony by jumping over a broom, another traditional marriage custom.

How long you stay tied together is also up to you—perhaps just for the length of your vows, or after the ceremony has finished.

Scrying with Fire
Divining the Wisdom of the Flames

Summer is the season of sun and fire. Gazing into fire and seeing spirits, messages, guides, faces, and otherworldly presences (also called pyromancy) is an accessible and fascinating portal to the wisdom of the divine and to the spirit world.

FLAME GAZING: Gazing into a candle flame or a pile of burning embers is a simple way to divine with fire. Sit in silence and in pitch darkness, other than the flame. Let your focus blur out and your mind clear of all chatter and thoughts.

Watch the flames and see what shapes, messages, or feelings come. You can also watch the flicker of the flames and the direction of the smoke, or listen to the sounds and rhythms as it burns.

SPIRIT SUMMONING: Ask to see a spirit guide's face in the fire — or ask directly for guidance and wisdom from the element of fire. This type of fire scrying can be intense — so always visualize an orb of white light around yourself first and ask for protective energy to guide you.

HERB CASTING: Cast dragon's blood resin into the fire and ask for guidance from your shadow side. Toss bay into the fire and look for a message from your divine self. Throw a handful of mugwort into the fire and request to see a creative vision.

ASH SCRYING: After your midsummer bonfire (or any ceremonial fire!), take a handful of cooled ashes and toss them onto the ground. Gaze to look for any shapes or patterns that emerge. You can also gaze at the ashes as they have fallen in the fire pit.

Your Own Battle of Light and Dark
Exploring The Wisdom of Contrast

The "battle of light and dark" is a potent theme in Litha's folklore. It may sound grandiose, but we all wage our own personal battles on this theme throughout life.

When our own personal seasons turn from light to darker times, it's important to remember that "darkness" is not a loss or a setback, but an inevitable and natural part of the cycle that can guide us forward. To honor this ebb and flow within your life, create a mandala of alternating dark and light items.

Prepare: Collect several "light" items (white flowers, quartz, bright herbs, sun symbols, etc.) and an equal number of "dark" items (black stones, night-blooming flowers, dark figurines, etc.) The number of items is up to you. Collect just enough to put into a circle, or more if you wish.

Cast the spell: Create your mandala by arranging the light and dark items in a circle or pattern to signify the wisdom found in both light and shadow. As you place the items, let them point to moments of joy and success and the contrasting times of struggle and stillness. How has the darkness brought you to light, and how has the light brought you to darkness? Both can guide your way.

Find a moment of peace and equal acceptance of dark and light. You'll know you're there when you feel a bit of a release and an understanding that all seasons serve a purpose. There is good in the bad, and bad in the good. This is a universal law.

Finish your ritual: Disassemble your mandala, scattering natural elements like flowers and herbs to the wind if you like.

Floromancy
Divining Omens from Flowers

Floromancy, also called flower scrying or flower divination, is a captivating practice that uses the mysticism of flowers to uncover messages and omens. It is a way of channeling earth energy and the elements of nature to tap into the wisdom that surrounds us all.

Select flowers that resonate with you personally. If you grew them in your own garden—even better! Choose flowers based on their symbolic meaning, or simply use what is available or attractive to you.

You might like to choose symbolic colors for the flowers you gather. Colors can enhance the divinatory meaning—red flowers might draw messages of vitality and courage, while yellow flowers could suggest joy and friendship.

Once you have your chosen flowers, there are many methods to use them to divine messages and answers from the wisdom of nature.

The "classic" and most well-known method is to pluck the petals off a flower while repeating alternate phrases, such as "they love me, they love me not." Whatever phrase the last petal is plucked on is the true answer.

Or scatter petals or small blooms and read them like tea leaves — cast them to the wind while focusing on a question. The pattern they form when they land can provide insights— perhaps pointing in a direction to take or forming a shape that holds meaning for you.

Another powerful form of floromancy is to simply gaze at the center of a flower until your mind clears and you reach a meditative state. In that trance, you will be connected to the source of divine wisdom, and you will receive the answers that you are seeking.

MOON ENERGY AND SPELL IDEAS

NEW & WAXING MOON: Increasing confidence, abundance, and making new friends.
FULL MOON: Protection, celebrating your success, and divination for your brightest self.
WANING & DARK MOON: Releasing self-doubt, perfectionism, and negative emotions.

*Sip ginger and citrus tea to ignite your spirit,
enliven your senses, and stoke the fire of action.*

EDIBLE FLOWERS

Sprinkle edible flower petals like calendula, borage, pansy, and nasturtium onto your salads to bring the magic of the wild into your meal.

Decorating for Litha
Celebrating The Beauty of Nature

Celebrate the warmth, light, and splendor of Litha with these enchanting decorative rituals.

Decorate your home with flowers and natural elements to beautify your space and bring the magic and energy of the season indoors.

Floral Displays: Choose bright, sun-loving flowers like sunflowers, marigolds, and daisies to create vibrant bouquets or garlands. These flowers symbolize the strength and power of the sun. Arrange them in central areas of your home to attract light and positivity.

Herb Wreaths: Craft wreaths from herbs such as lavender, rosemary, and thyme. Hang your wreath on the front door to ward off negative energy and invite peace into your home, or place them over your altar or mantle. The scent and sight of these herbal creations will imbue your home with magic.

Stone Circles or Labyrinths: Arrange stones or crystals on your altar or in your garden. This will act as a miniature henge, focusing solar energies to the earth. Light a candle in the center to symbolize the sun.

Water Features: Incorporate bowls of water with floating flowers and candles, or dedicate a fountain or birdbath as a centerpiece of your Litha decorations. Using water elements can help to balance the fiery energy of the sun.

Solar Crosses: Create a sunwheel (also called a solar cross) using sticks and strings. Use it as a focus for your Litha ritual to symbolize the turning of the seasons and the Wheel of the Year.

By incorporating natural decorations and simple rituals into your home, you'll deepen your connection to the magical energies of the longest day of the year.

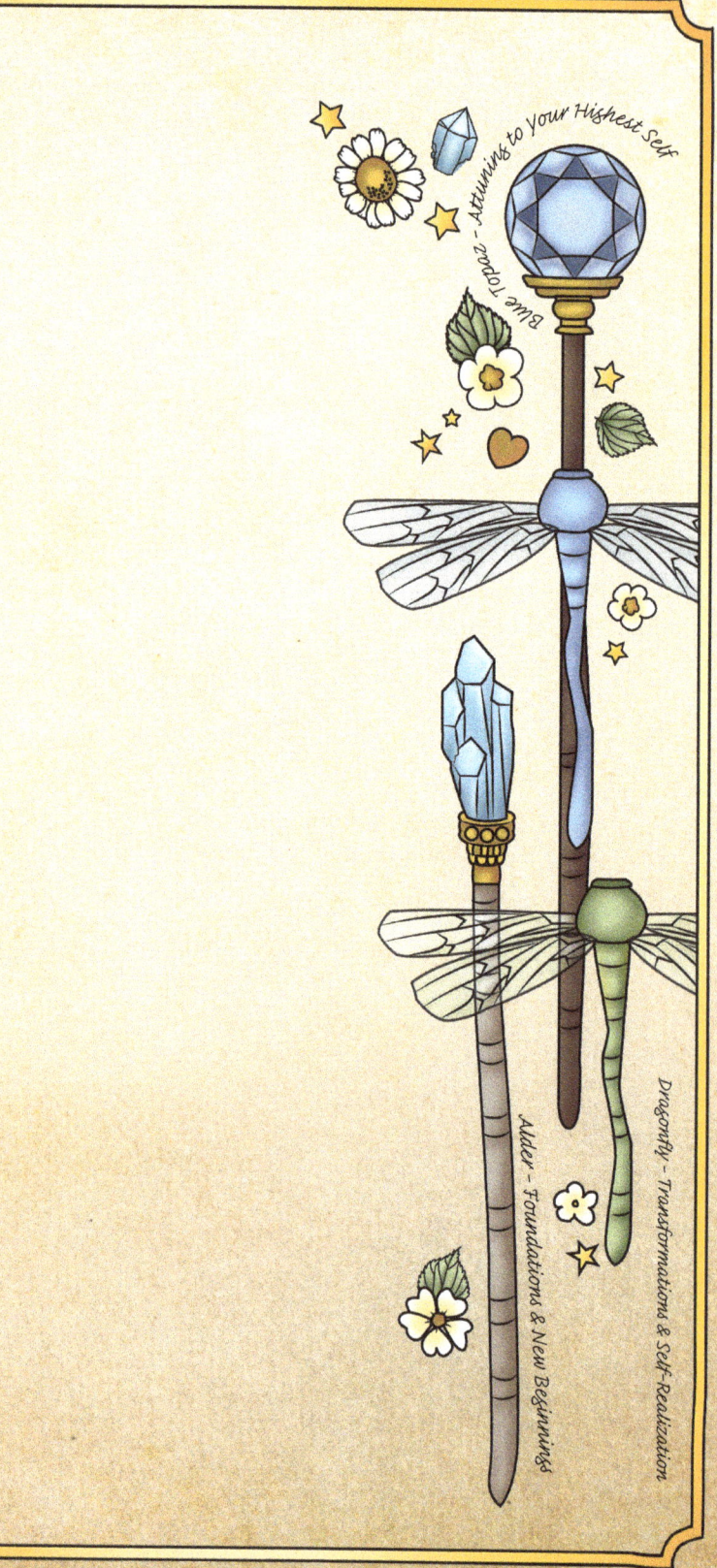

Litha Crafts
Solstice Wands
Empower Yourself with a Handmade Wand

The summer solstice is an "in-between" time of shifting seasons, and a chance to slip into another world, change your future, and rise to your full power.

It's also an excellent day to make or consecrate a wand. Traditionally, a witch would go in search of her wand's wood before dawn and follow specific customs. (Research if you want to do this in the old ways, otherwise, create your wand as you see fit.) You can use a crystal wand, a metal scepter, something you bought, something you made, or whatever you like.

Things You'll Need: Your wand. A ritual fire or cauldron with sand at the bottom and three yellow candles within. Chamomile or fennel tea. Dragon's blood, bay, pine, or cinquefoil incense.

Perform the Ritual: Place your wand out in the full noon sun on the solstice for at least three hours or until sunset. If it's a crystal wand, make sure it is made from sun-safe crystals.

Then light your cauldron or candles. Wield your wand skyward and with power as you circle the flames thirteen times, clockwise. If you have a fire, you can cast flowers or herbs into the fire. If you are using the candles, just toss a bit of herbs towards the flames as you go 'round. Meanwhile, chant (or words of your choosing):

May this witch and wand acquire
The power of this solstice fire.

As the fire burns out, sit and sip mead or chamomile tea. Pick out tarot cards that symbolize the brightest version of "you," or gaze into the flames and embers for intuitive wisdom.

Sweep in the energy of abundance with a broom made from wheat straw or vervain.

Litha Crafts
Solstice Brooms
Craft and Empower Your Ritual Broom

Decorate your broom with seashells to add protective qualities.

The summer solstice is a powerful time to craft or enchant a ritual broom, also called a besom. Traditionally used in cleansing and protective rituals to "sweep out" unwanted energy, your broom can also be a tool of empowerment to "sweep in" what you desire. Use natural elements like flowers, essential oils, and different types of wood to enchant your broom with magical qualities.

If you're making a broom from scratch, select a wood that resonates with your personal intentions. Birch is ideal for new beginnings, ash for protection, and oak for strength and stability.

Twigs from trees like willow or hazel are traditional bristle choices and add flexibility and resilience. You can also work with dried herbal sprigs such as lavender for peace and protection or rosemary for purification.

Tie a small bouquet of fresh or dried flowers around the handle. Change up these adornments seasonally, using whatever grows in your garden or feels intentionally relevant to you. For the summer solstice, try St. John's wort or a brilliant sunflower.

Anointing with Oils: Essential oils can be used to anoint your broom, imbuing it with additional energies and magical scents. Citrus oils energize and cleanse, while floral scents like ylang-ylang or rose uplift and open the heart. Apply a few drops to the handle or bristles while focusing on your intentions.

Consecration of the Sun: On the solstice, take your broom outdoors at noon. Hold it up to the sun and "charge" your broom with the sun's power, consecrating and powering it up for use in your spells and rituals.

Feather Colors

Blue - Peace
Green - Prosperity
Yellow - Happiness
Brown - Stability
Red - Strength
Black & White - Balance
Grey - Psychic Awareness
White - Purity and Light
Black - Knowledge

Witch's Ladder
A Charm for Protection or other Workings

Crafting a charm of protection and strength is a classic summer solstice activity among witches.

You can also work intentions of abundance, life, fertility, love, wishes, or anything else you want to power up with the sun's sacred light.

Make a traditional Witch's Ladder by braiding three 3-foot strands of yarn (red, white, and black). Then sew an odd number of feathers in symbolic colors, evenly spaced, along the length of the braid. Tie the ends of the braid together so it forms a circle. Feel free to chant a rhyme or a witchy poem while you braid, and keep your intention in your mind as you craft it.

If you want to get fancier or more creative, you can use different colors of yarn and feathers, or add beads, charms, sprigs of herbs, or other symbolic embellishments for your intentions.

Create your charm a few weeks before the solstice. At noon on the solstice day, perform this simple spell with your witch's ladder to enchant it with the power of the sun.

Place your charm outside at noon. Sprinkle salt on it to purify, then say your intentions for protection, strength, abundance, or whatever you've chosen. Keep your charm outside for at least three hours or until sundown. If you are lighting a bonfire or candle spell at sundown, you can also pass your charm over the ritual flame to enhance the power of the spell.

Flower Crowns
Adorn Yourself For Midsummer Celebrations

If you like to get crafty, create flower crowns to adorn yourself and your loved ones. Flower and green crowns, garlands, bouquets, and fruit centerpieces are all easy to make and a fun way to channel the energy of the season. And you can mix the flowers, herbs, and other elements to concoct a spell with their magical properties.

To make crowns or garlands, you'll need grapevine wire (sold at any craft store), green floral tape, flowers, herbs, leaves, vines, small crystal points, and anything else you want to put on your crown. Or, use the traditional flower weaving method on the next page. You can also use silk flowers so your crown will last for many years, then add fresh sprigs of herbs seasonally to re-enchant and freshen it up on each solstice.

Try making your crown of vibrant yellow flowers and blooms like roses or St. John's wort to symbolize the power of the sun. Lavender is an excellent herb choice for making summer crowns. Check online (and the next page) for lots of great tutorials, videos, and inspiration on making crowns and garlands if you need more instructions, but here are the basics:

Cut a length of wire large enough to wrap around your head three or four times. It's best to make it a little big and then pinch it to fit. Form the wire into a whimsical, uneven "wreath" type shape that will fit on your head comfortably. Secure the wreath shape with floral tape in two or three places, making sure to stretch the tape so it gets sticky and holds. Then start adding flowers by attaching the stems with floral tape and overlapping them as you go around.

Create a crown from herbs and flowers like basil, mint, fruit blossom, and cloves to manifest abundance.

HOW TO WEAVE A FLOWER CROWN

1. Gather some flowers with long stems. Place one flower on top of another.

2. Wrap one stem over the other, under it, then around itself.

3. As you loop and weave them together, keep the stems going the same way.

4. Add more flowers one by one using the same method.

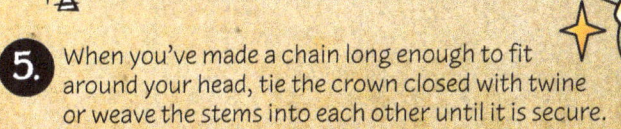

5. When you've made a chain long enough to fit around your head, tie the crown closed with twine or weave the stems into each other until it is secure.

About the Artist

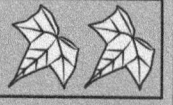

Amy is an author and illustrator who loves animated musicals. She also likes watercolor painting, witchcraft, and walking on the beach in a really big sun hat.

Not only does she own every Nintendo game console ever made, she's earned several fancy diplomas and enjoys continued studies in various magical practices.

CONTACT AMY AND SEE MORE BOOKS, PRINTABLE PAGES, AND ART:
Amy@ColoringBookofShadows.com
ColoringBookofShadows.com

©2025 Amy Cesari, Book of Shadows LLC

www.ingramcontent.com/pod-product-compliance
Lightning Source LLC
Chambersburg PA
CBHW050730010526
44107CB00009B/797